Why I Decided Not to Kill Myself

Kent Philpott

EVP
Earthen Vessel Publishing

Why I Decided Not to Kill Myself

©2023 by Kent Philpott

All rights reserved.
Earthen Vessel Media, LLC
San Rafael, CA 94903
www.earthenvesselmedia.com.com

ISBN: 978-1-946794-40-6
Interior design by KLC Philpott

No part of this publication may be reproduced, stored in a retrieval system, or transmitted in any form or by any means, electronic or mechanical, including photocopying, recording, or by any information retrieval system, without the written permission of the author or publisher, except by a reviewer who wishes to quote brief passages in connection with a review written for inclusion in a magazine, newspaper, internet site, or broadcast.

All Biblical Scripture quotations, unless otherwise indicated, are taken from the Holy Bible, English Standard Version® (ESV®), copyright © 2001 by Crossway Bibles, a publishing ministry of Good News Publishers. All rights reserved.

Contents

Introduction and Reasons Why and Why Not	7
Are you perhaps a Hamlet?	15
"Kent will go insane or commit suicide within a year"	18
Too embarrassed about what I have done to face the world anymore	21
I am all alone	23
I often feel guilty . . .	26
Is it advisable to talk . . . ?	29
Please forgive me for sinning against you.	31
Forgiveness: the Great Miracle	32
How would others be impacted if I killed myself?	34
Their Stories	37
Concluding Thoughts	42

Introduction: Reasons Why and Why Not

How many of us think about killing ourselves? I am going to guess that the majority of the people on the planet will sometimes fall into this mode.

For those who do, let me just say that it is important to face it, to admit, not only to yourself but to others.

Should you be embarrassed about thinking of killing yourself?

If you do think about it, does this make you a bad person or a huge failure?

In preparation for writing this booklet, I sent out a letter to a host of people asking their opinion about the subject of the book. Several hundred went out to alumni of our Divorce Recovery Workshop. The result was dozens of letters coming in expressing thoughts, and these are categorized here. Following is the substance of the letter I sent out.

Taking stock of your situation:

1. Explain in the space below how you are feeling right now.
2. Sum up in three sentences, why you have decided to kill yourself.
3. Make a list of the persons who would be impacted by your suicide.

4. Make a list of any persons you can think of who might be moved toward killing themselves after hearing of your own suicide.
5. Would some of them even blame themselves?
6. What needs to change in order for you to drop the notion of wanting to kill yourself?
7. What events brought you to this place?

I have placed the responses into two categories.

Some reasons why:

A TRAUMA

Things happen to us. A parent dies while we are young. An injury occurs that impacts significantly. A brother or sister is accidentally killed. Someone sexually molests us. A mentally disturbed parent treats us badly. We witness bloodshed and other miseries while growing up. We do not make the team or get kicked off one for legitimate reasons or not. A teacher, a priest, a minister, a doctor, a neighbor, or fill in the blank _____, violates our sacred trust. Maybe we fall in with the wrong crowd and end up spending time locked up, maybe a long time locked up.

Perhaps we end up in the military and our minds get tweaked. Nothing in our lives, even football, prepares us for the trauma of living with death and mayhem every day. Even if injury is avoided, still just being around the confusion results in circumstances we can't control. Maybe it is fear that grabs a hold, maybe anger. If you see enough death and destruction, especially of buddies, anger is going to be there. Fear or anger or both, if suppressed, is going to do serious damage.

Dreams can be diminished if not crushed completely. Hopes of a happy life seem to fly away. A spouse, a family, a chance to live as we thought of as kids—so much is taken away and often irrevocably so. Whether we were at the wrong place at the wrong time or, as is often the case, we have no one to blame but ourselves, we come away with reasons to kill ourselves for the traumas that have settled upon us.

A LOSS OF RELATIONSHIP

I have been through divorce; it was the worst experience of my life without question, and I have not yet gotten over it and I never will completely. Much of it was my fault, and the pain it has caused others, especially my kids, never leaves me.

For over 35 years I have conducted a divorce recovery and loss workshop. Many hundreds of people have been through the eight-week workshop. Over the years I have seen people struggle with their losses, and I mean mightily, and to the best of my knowledge we have never lost anyone to suicide.

However, statistics show that 90% of all who go through loss of a love relationship, whether due to divorce, separation, death of a spouse—any kind of ending—consider suicide. I can attest to that both personally and as the result of leading the loss workshop all these years.

On the opening night of each workshop, I make it clear that recovery can be expected. People start crying. They cannot imagine that they will ever recover any semblance of their former selves, and I can see on their faces, or so I think, that they are telling themselves, "Everyone else might recover, but I won't." Then I tell them how long I have been doing the workshop and that I can confidently say, despite how very crappy someone feels now, with work and pain, there will be a large measure of recovery.

Loss hits our emotions. There is guilt, rejection, fear, anger, loneliness, and much more, and these can be quite raw emotional experiences. When we love someone, it is a big deal, and when that love is lost it can be overwhelmingly awful. Our emotional health is immediately compromised and we don't think clearly. Sometimes all we can think of is that we want out of it all—all the memories, all the anger and hurt, all the bleak future images. There is recovery even when we imagine it is impossible.

Approach of incapacity

Life is risky. Our first reason, trauma, can result in a physical or mental incapacity.

A friend developed Parkinson's disease. A vibrant, strong man with many irons in the fire, then suddenly, home bound and trapped in a body that wasn't working right.

Another acquaintance suffered a benign brain tumor, and after surgery to remove it, he found he was incapable of performing simple tasks and so had to be placed in a group home. He was still intelligent in most of the ways he had been when he ran a very successful service related business. But how shattered he was when he realized he could not do math anymore, so essentially his working days were over. And he was in his mid-forties, at the peak of his career.

A member of my congregation was a biker, and as usually happens, he hit the road one day—hit it hard. That ended much of what he could do, including take care of his wife and children. He went through hell on this and very nearly did not make it.

Just one more: a dear woman, working in an elderly care facility, living alone but loving the work of caring for people in need, accidentally hit her head on a lead pipe, and the injury compromised her brain function. She had to go on a form of welfare as a result. What a crushing blow it was for her.

Physical impairment, mental incapacity—it would be natural to consider suicide. Life forever altered and no going back; people do go on though, yes they do and find that they are glad they did

Discouragement and Depression

Discouragement and depression are likely related, and I do not know where one starts and the other begins. Discouragement I know about; maybe there was some actual depression present as well, but the point is, I was feeling very bad about myself and my life.

In my years visiting and coaching at San Quentin, I have talked with many convicts who fought discouragement like they were in a gang war. Gang members do a crime and get a long sentence. I have seen a few young guys, mixed up in a gang, though sometimes there was no alternative, no choice in the matter, who got a fifty-years-to-life sentence while in their early twenties. Somewhat discouraging! No bleeding heart here, and I did not go on about the injustices in the prison system, but suicide often seems like the only way to go, and soon I hear the person is locked away on suicide watch.

In dealing with convicts I have learned it does no one any good to make victims out of them. They did their crime, and now they are doing time, and it must be so. People who hurt or otherwise prey on people have to be removed from a society that determines to live in peace and security, but that does not mean suicide is ever something to ignore or become callous about. Life is life, and I have figured out that it is only by the grace of God and the nature of circumstances that I am not the one in the cell.

Discouragement is like a stealth emotion—we may not know we are being impacted by it. We become easily frustrated, little things become big things, we blow up over insignificant events, we hibernate, close down, don't want to go places and be with people, and the list goes on. We become discouraged, and friends don't help; their suggestions and advice are little more than irritants.

Over time our world gets smaller and smaller. If we read the newspapers and watch the television news broadcasts, the whole world seems submerged in a thick brown soup. The discouragement clings tightly and thoughts of killing ourselves look better and better. What a surprise!

Dramatic reversal of life circumstances

My friend lived in a nice home and had a good paying job. He played golf, had a neat old car, and then was diagnosed with head and neck cancer. Without going into details, which are essentially irrelevant, he lost almost everything. Once there was money, now only SSI; the tricked out roadster had to be sold; no strength for golf anymore; food had no flavor; no more sex even if the wife hadn't left him; and he was living in a studio apartment after he had to sell his rather grand house to pay the medical bills. All in a period of about two years. Dramatic reversal of life circumstances—indeed.

The money ran out, life style changed, no job, domicile ugly, no toys, no prospects, few if any friends—suicide? Of course the thought goes through the mind.

Another one: He got involved with a weird association of churches that were into wild Pentecostal worship and gatherings. He ended up mortgaging his house in order to purchase for the group a new, almost resort-like worship edifice, but the minister ran off with the money and the secretary, leaving everyone holding a large and smelly bag. He had spent years as an alcoholic, had found Jesus, genuinely and sincerely, also found this church, and his life was looking up. And then. He did not fall off the wagon, but he compensated, took up rich foods and lots of it, gained one hundred or more pounds, had a heart attack, developed diabetis—that's enough to eventually start thinking of suicide.

He wanted to live, just a little. He went to AA, found a new church, joined a gym, stopped going to the fast food joints, and still though of suicide. He tried it, but clumsily, and got counseling. He is alive, and I am confident he will make it. But barely.

Here are other "Whys" that you can fill in with stories of people you know or that you are experiencing yourself:

FEAR OF A LONG, PAINFUL DEATH

BEING REJECTED BY PEOPLE I LOVE

NOT CARING ANYMORE

Now, some reasons why not:

1. Don't give your enemies the satisfaction.
2. People who love you will be hurt.
3. People who don't even know you will be impacted.
4. There are some options you haven't considered.

Then three questions need to be asked but don't need to be answered:

1. What needs to change in order for you to drop the notion of wanting to kill yourself?
2. Is suicide murder?
3. Will I be condemned to hell if I kill myself?

Let me clarify something here. I have been a pastor now for 52 years, and during the earliest of these years, I ran the Marin Counseling Center. (In my college years my major was psychology). I found that my work centered on encouraging counselees to talk about what they were going through. And just being able to get the inner pain out made a huge difference. This is precisely what I am attempting to do here.

An important conclusion

Before moving on to a few more stories, I want to be point out to the reader that the responses I received were from people who decided not to kill themselves. In varying ways, they found a way out. Somehow, a reason to live sustained them. Problems were solved, accommodations were made, hope was discovered, treatment was received, hearts and minds were calmed, and they lived to tell their stories so that others might do the same. And you are invited to tell your story of why you decided not to kill yourself. Write it out, however imperfectly, short or long, and send it along.

Here is my email address, in case a reader is also struggling to stay alive:

kentphilpott@comcast.net

Please include a phone number, and if you leave a message, I will get back to you as soon as I can.

1
Are you perhaps a Hamlet?

Hamlet was depressed, and seriously so.

His father, the king of Denmark, had been murdered by his uncle, the king's brother. If that loss were not enough, the uncle, now the king, took Hamlet's newly widowed mother as his wife.

The whole sordid affair plays on Hamlet's mind, especially the way his mother has behaved. She quickly "moved on" and wed, without knowing it was to his father's murderer. Hamlet is soured on women and marriage in general. His feelings of love for Ophelia, to whom he has already given his love, has become a source of anguish for the young man, so much so that he will say to her: "Get thee to a nunnery: why wouldst thou be a breeder of sinners?"

Hamlet is desperate; he does not know what to do. He has learned about the truth of his father's murder by the ghost of his father. This is not the sort of evidence that can be brought to light and believed. Hamlet feels absolutely alone and very angry.

Not seeing any way out of his torment, he contemplates suicide. If he could simply cease to exist—that might be the answer. So then, he utters the famous words, "To be, or not to be; that is the question"—perhaps Shakespeare's most repeated verse. If he could only die, sleep, be no more, then the heartaches, the shocks, and all the suffering humans are prone to experience might vanish.

But his mind will not let him off that easily. There is the possibility he might dream—and this thought gives him pause.

> *"The dread of something after death,*
> *The undiscovered country, from whose bourn*
> *No traveler returns, puzzles the will,*
> *And makes us rather bear those ills we have*
> *Than fly to others that we know not of..."*

Hamlet's question of whether it is better to live or die is one nearly all human beings will ask themselves. I have. Perhaps you have. Perhaps you know someone whom you suspect might be thinking along such tragic lines.

BROTHER GARY

My brother Gary came back from the war in Vietnam wounded in mind and spirit. What he experienced as a combat engineer there in the year 1968 robbed him of his ability to work through his pain. Though his other brother and I and our parents sought to encourage him and give him new hope, we failed, or rather we were not able to break through to the place he had gone to hide, and one morning he drove his Volkswagen Beatle to a nearby Lutheran hospital in the San Fernando Valley, parked under an American flag, and shot himself in the head. While my other brother Bruce was alive, we could still become immersed in sadness discussing the suicide of our beloved little brother many decades earlier.

The sorrow of that event, mixed with many other suicides I have come to know as a pastor of churches, is the reason I am writing this book. The killing of oneself is all too common. It seems we read of one in the newspapers every day. Perhaps it is not epidemic, but it is common. And we must speak of it; it must come to the light so that it is in some way stripped of its power.

Let's talk about it

If people can talk about their feelings of suicide, it may be a step away from the pain and hopelessness that most often lie behind the desire to kill oneself. It seemed to me that a book with such a title as this one might be useful. It seemed to me that if I could find some people who were willing to talk about why they decided not to kill themselves, when they in fact had seriously contemplated doing just that, it might be incorporated into a book that would be believable, a book I would feel good about giving to others who are in a desperate place.

2
"Kent will go insane or commit suicide within a year"

This "prophecy" was given by a woman whom I had helped and encouraged through a troubled marriage over a period of years. Now, one week after my resignation from the charismatic church where I was senior pastor in San Rafael, California, this same woman made her pronouncement from the pulpit, while my teenage daughter sat in the congregation. The pastor who then replaced me announced that my entire family was to be shunned from that point on. This, again, while my eldest daughter was present. The year was 1980.

My dear daughter came home in tears and told me what had happened. I was determined from that point on to keep from going crazy. And I would certainly not kill myself. (I ran into this very woman some years later, and she denied having made the statement. My guess is that she was disappointed that her "word from God" had not come true.)

Not that I did not think of killing myself on several occasions—I did. Going through the divorce was pure hell, and all these years later I have not completely recovered, but I would never give that false prophet or her eager hearers the satisfaction of seeing her predictions come true. Is this a bad motivation?

No satisfaction for my enemies

There it is—reason #1 for not killing myself. Whether it is the healthiest of reasons does not matter to me. Sure, I have a number of other reasons, which I will get to as this book proceeds, but #1 worked at the time and continues to serve me well.

I have always had enemies of one variety or another. Some I may have imagined; others were real. They were not the kind of enemies with whom I might fight it out with bare knuckles, but enemies, nevertheless.

There are some people, sad to say, who would like to see me dead. This is no doubt true for many of us. But I am not going to give them the satisfaction. Not at all. There is no question that I have failed people, let people down, and abused trust put in me. And I can feel pretty bad about it. Oh well! Whether these people learn grace and forgiveness is not my problem; I have forgiven myself as best I can, despite the fact I cannot forget; I have been forgiven by God, so I refuse to live a life of guilt and shame.

There is a saying I like to remind myself of from time to time: "The devil is an accuser." That is not all the quote but enough to tell me I have another enemy, unseen and flying below the radar. And I am not going to give that bastard any satisfaction, either. Another point about the devil: he has been "a murderer from the beginning," and that was spoken by Jesus who would know.

A murderer from the beginning. That enemy—I refuse to satisfy him either. No, I am going to live and fight back.

Before getting into some of the stories from others, I wanted to open up with my own experience so you can see this is not merely an academic treatise. No, I am more than an observer—I am a player. I have been there, as they say, and I have something to contribute, since I have actually been through *two* divorces, and that is enough to drive anyone to the bridge, I mean the Golden Gate Bridge, which is just a short distance down Highway 101. I also have five kids, eight grand kids, and three great-grand kids. But more than that, I have been a pastor of three churches for the last fifty-plus years. Right, I am an old dude now (almost wrote dud), but I am still here and going strong, even though I have felt like giving it all up on any number of occasions—discouraged, probably depressed, angry, and saddened all at once, with the thought of killing myself stealing across the brain and lodging in the heart.

Mostly, I have dummied up about my feelings and would never think of talking to a therapist. I haven't even talked to my closest friends about my dark times. I am mostly an upbeat, type-A guy, and those who know me would be shocked to learn I have even felt bad enough to think of suicide. Not that I sink down into that pit, but I have looked over the edge. Come on, most of us have peered over at one time or another. It is really nothing that needs to be hidden. On the contrary, the whole subject has to be brought out into the open.

So, I admit it. Does it make me a bad person, or a sick person, or a person to be avoided, or to be pampered, if I have thought about killing myself? No, maybe it is better to engage with those who can take me like I am. The rest can hang with those who are balanced, focused, purpose-driven success stories who skip lightly over the mountain tops and never slip into a valley.

3
Too embarrassed about what I have done to face the world anymore

I have experienced this sensation a number of times, but somehow over the years, it has been fading away. The reality is, So what! It is now not enough to get me to think I need to do myself in.

Forgiveness—the reality is that I do know, though not really feel, that my sin has been forgiven—past, present, and future. I also know that the enemy of Christ, and therefore of myself, throws this at me from time to time. And it stinks for sure. But slowly, I have been able to ignore this and say to myself, "Yeah Philpott, you are the worst that has ever been, yet I know of the incredible power of God to wash my sin away. So, get behind me Satan."

I am thinking now of folks who are saying, "Okay, good for Kent, but I am not there yet." Here is where we need to ignore our feelings and focus and center on the finished work of Christ. We cling to truth not to feelings and emotions.

Of course, there will be times when someone, whether intentionally or accidentally or unintentionally, will bring up our sinning. It happened to me three days ago, and at church for that matter. It was unintentional, said jokingly, but I heard it, and for a moment I was angry. Yes, there I was, Pastor Kent, and the words were heard. What did I do? I laughed right along with the others. It even went through my mind that I hoped the person who uttered the gaff was going to be okay.

How many of such incidents have I endured? Too many to count.

Am I still embarrassed about some of the things I have done? Yes, I am, but this is not enough to think about killing myself. Yes, years ago this is what would hit me, but I am moving away from this now. Thank God for His mercy.

4
I am all alone

For reasons I am unaware of, I am mostly alone. I work out of my house, when I can find work, so no co-workers, etc., just alone day after day. Sure, I see some of the folks living around me, but no real contact. Earlier in my life, I had family and some friends. I doubt I will ever marry; no one has really ever been interested in me. I confess that I cry about this a lot. It makes me want to end it all.

The above is a composite of life experiences that I have heard from people over the years, and I could go on further with it, but I think it is plain where I am going.

Being lonely is now recognized as a national pandemic-like circumstance. A high percentage of Americans live alone, and this number is climbing. It is noted that all ages are represented, too—young, middle aged, and old folks like me.

Some can barely make it outside of the places they live, often due to physical conditions, so time goes rolling along in aloneness. And the thought of ending it all takes hold, and this is not uncommon at all.

As a pastor of a church, thankfully a small congregation, I am aware of those who are virtually living alone and without much contact with others. Not too long ago an elderly lady here at Miller Avenue Church went missing and it took several weeks before we found that she had died of a heart attack in her home, and no one knew. Yes, I lay some blame for this on myself, as have several others at MAC. In fact, we are spreading her ashes three days from the writing of this piece.

My heart aches from time to time when I realize the unhappy conditions some are living with. I think the primary ministry I engage in is phone calling. I have a sheet of paper with 29 names on it, and it is my goal to call each of these at least every other week. It could be the most important thing I do. There are at least six of those on my list who have never attended a church service and likely never will.

Aloneness, then, is not one of the factors which has troubled me over the years; actually a little less contact would be fine, but what happens to me is that my heart aches for the lonely ones.

"Only the lonely," so the song goes, sung by Roy Orbison, and it is the lonely ones I so much want to focus on. First things first then: those of us who are lonely have to admit that we are lonely and figure out ways to deal with it. Wow, what a potent thing to reveal: "Hi my name is Kent, and I am lonely."

Here are some ideas, and I know I am only scratching the surface:

Find a place to meet with other people. Katie and I are pastors, so we have our congregation that we spend hours with every week. Seek out a church—a small one is good— and get to know folks. Get involved, if at all possible. Sing in a choir, be an usher, volunteer to do janitorial tasks, go to a Bible study class or a women's group or a men's group, and the list of options can be quite long. Talk to a pastor, an elder, or a deacon, and be frank about your situation. Good things could happen.

If not a church, then maybe a community center of some kind. We are members of our local Jewish Community Center, and we have lots of friends there. In fact, about half the time we spend there is in talking with others. So, we have two good, healthy activities there: working out and meeting people.

Most communities have things going on that a person could engage in. Look around, go on the internet (places like Meetup.com), check out local newspapers—you will find some groups to be part of. Don't give up, keep searching, make the calls. Other ideas are working with animals, a gardener's guild, a bridge club.

Another possibility is to contact a social worker by calling your county's administrative office and explaining your need. Also think about contacting your local school district office to find out if they need volunteers. Volunteers are needed in so many non-profit and public service arenas, so check with your local city or county for the contact info.

Get involved, do something, and do not give up easily. There will be a place where you are needed, even if the need can be met over the internet or a phone line.

We simply will not allow loneliness to kill us. No way!

5
I often feel guilty . . .

I often feel guilty when I am with others who know what kind of person I have been.

I wish this was not true of me, but I have to admit this is so. For years now, I have avoided those who knew full well what a jerk I have been. However, now that I am easing up on this guiltiness, I have even mentioned this in recent sermons.

Yes, two weeks ago, on the last Sunday in April of 2023, I mentioned one of my divorces and how badly I felt about it, even to the point of resigning from the church I now pastor and disappearing into the world. I was amazed as two people, one man and one woman, looked intently at me and nodded their heads in agreement. I knew both of their pasts, and I think it was a relief for them to hear this from me, especially from the pulpit.

I wonder how many people there are like me who could no longer face a congregation who knew the truth. Okay, I know it may be argued that it is better to keep silent, but then again, maybe not.

Is it not true that all have sinned? And I am not talking about only our pre-Christian lives, but our ongoing lives as well.

This reminds me of what happened with those who were followers of John Wesley, founder of the Methodist church movement, when toward the close of his life he said it was possible to live a sinless life. That then spawned the holiness movement. It was not long before some of the ordained leaders of this off-shoot of Methodism failed. Indeed, some of the leaders proved they were not all that holy, and though the history is convoluted and complex, it spawned the Pentecostal movement. Therefore, the great gift of the Holy Spirit morphed into speaking in tongues. In my opinion, this was a step in the right direction.

Some may say, well Philpott, you are giving out a license to sin or you are saying that it is not a big deal if a Christian, especially a Christian leader, sins. Absolutely not! We are called to walk in the footsteps of Jesus and flee from sin—and especially for those of us called to the work. Yet, I know that I am not without blame; I know I am vulnerable to attack. Yes, I face temptation each and every day. Most of the time I am able to turn away from sin, and I am not talking about the big stuff, but little stuff like tooting my own horn, exaggerating something I did or claiming something I did not do or was only a part of, making excuses to avoid difficulties, failing to follow through on ministry to someone I knew needed encouragement, not pouring myself into the preparation for the Sunday sermon, showing my anger before knowing all the circumstances, and on and on I could go.

Do I ever have sexual temptation? Certainly, I do, since that goes with the territory. While it is not active sin, it could be a step in the wrong direction. Porn—hmmm—is anyone reading this guilty here? A large percentage of Christian men in particular, but also women, have been lured into and engage in viewing it. It is a powerful and twisted impulse. Every so often, a man (almost always) feels safe enough with me to tell me of his compulsion. A case of this occurred two and half weeks ago. Porn addiction is probably one of the major stumbling blocks we face today. More are messed up over perverse sexuality than ever before. It stares one in the face daily and beckons over the internet and via social media apps.

1 Peter 5:8 is a verse that has been on my mind for a couple of years now: "Be sober-minded; be watchful. Your adversary the devil prowls around like a roaring lion, seeking someone to devour." Based on plentiful pastoral experience, I have come to see that the one who insists he or she is not vulnerable is the most likely target—in fact, the most vulnerable.

Indeed, we have to tell ourselves the truth. We have to admit our weaknesses and be quick to ask our gracious Lord and also those whom we might have harmed for forgiveness.

It is no simple thing to be a follower of Jesus in this sin-scarred world of ours. We are called to be honest with ourselves, with others, and the God to whom we pray.

6
Is it advisable to talk . . . ?

Is it advisable to talk with friends and family about past troubling events?

This is a difficult question indeed. Yes and No would have to be the answer. Yes, when it is safe, and No, when it may not be.

When would it not be safe? Perhaps this would be when the listener is not emotionally and spiritually strong enough to hear what might be unpleasant. A few times when I was much younger, it hurt me to hear about events that involved close family members. I needed to know these things, I guess, but it impacted me negatively. I would say that there are some things that should go unreported.

There have been times in my life when I had to shut up about problems I knew about family members. Just sitting here in front of my computer has brought a couple of instances rolling through my mind. Sometimes it might be better just to let things ride. While it might bring some relief to divulge, damage to others could be the result. I am suggesting that there be time spent in prayer, and careful consideration taken before making decisions about what to reveal and to whom.

So, the "no" part is complicated. Actually, it is all complicated. I am uncertain of how strong or deliberate to be here.

Concluding this brief piece, let me say that one needs to be careful about revealing that which might best be forgotten and hidden. Based on my years engaged in counseling, both as a therapist and a pastor, revelations of a serious nature might do more harm than good.

However, I can also easily state, that if someone has a need to talk about past events, it is advisable to go to a professional or to someone who is not connected to the events. Over more than 52 years as a pastor now, I have heard many an unhappy story that needed to be brought into the light of day but without going any further.

We may have to sit on tales that could still cause pain, and I think this is what maturity is about—the strength to know the horrors of past events but turn the pain over to our Lord who is always ready to listen. Yes, He is the great counselor.

7
Please forgive me for sinning against you.

I wrapped up chapter six regarding talking with others about emotional, even spiritual pain in the past. Now this is a bit different.

To start with, I have done this very thing—asking someone I harmed in the past to forgive me, and to be honest, I am experiencing some unpleasant emotions right now. I recall a time or two when I was glad I made the confession and asked for forgiveness, but then I did not adequately calculate the repercussions that caused further harm.

To engage someone whom we have damaged in some way in the process of confession and requesting forgiveness requires careful consideration. For one thing, we must be sure we are doing this for the other person's sake and not our own. It is not enough just to get things off one's chest, so to speak. Our concern is for the other person who has been sinned against.

Some examples: A person who has been cheated financially, taken sexual advantage of, defamed due to rumors or lies, ignored or rejected under difficult circumstances, promised something but ignored with loss following, and many other circumstances of being harmed are some of the acceptable conditions for requesting forgiveness. However, asking for forgiveness might possibly open up the wounds again. Sometimes ignored and forgotten is best.

But, and this is a big but, asking forgiveness can go a long way to healing relationships gone awry.

8
Forgiveness: the Great Miracle

Recently, I wrote a book about how I had made "shipwreck" of my faith and my life, and this term was based on something the Apostle Paul said in 1 Timothy 1:18–19.

I confess I have contemplated suicide from time to time—no actual attempts—but the thoughts brought on a depressed state of mind. And during the pandemic we learned about S.A.D., Seasonal Attitudinal Disorder. I had it, mostly all gone now, since we are in the Spring of the year, but I did not hide it from others. The result was a number of them telling me they felt the same way.

Once again, I have to admit that my two divorces yet haunt me; I was not the sole trouble, but enough to impact my life as I think back over those times. No question but that I was a "bad man." And some of those who knew me, even other ministers and pastors, rejected me then and continue to do so to this day.

How I faced the really stupid and rebellious things I have done made all the difference. And this is because I came to a greater understanding of the forgiveness I have in my Lord Jesus Christ and the personal admission that I am not as wonderful as I would like to be.

I have to explain a paradox here, due to two Greek words that are found in the New Testament, and both of these are translated by the word "time." They are kairos and chronos (transliterations from the Greek to the English). Kairos is God's time; chronos is human time, dependent on the rotating earth traveling around the sun.

And here is the saving grace: my sin, and all of it—past, present, and future—was placed upon Jesus on the cross. This is kairos time, and it is in kairos time where God is. Chronos time—ongoing, day by day—is where I am and in which I sin.

Let me say it another way: my sin, even that yet in the future, was laid upon Jesus on that "Good Friday" so long ago. Yes, the sin of all those who trust in Jesus as their Savior and to whom the Holy Spirit reveals the truth and does the saving work, from the beginning of creation to the very end, the whole of that sin is covered in the shed blood of the Lamb of God.

Only the Creator God could do this, and of course we cannot grasp it all. Some argue that this point of Biblical theology gives us an excuse to continue to sin. Yet the paradox of time stands clearly in the Bible.

I do not sin that grace might more abound, as the old saying goes. It is knowing that our sin is covered that inspires us to more closely follow Jesus and turn from sin. To live in this crazy world is often horrid, and there is great relief in knowing that my sin is covered and I belong to Him forever.

This great miracle then gives us the courage to live on. This does not mean that I don't get down from time to time, I do, but I remind myself of the salvation I have, and I have an inner strength, brought by the working of the Holy Spirit, that gives me the desire to keep on keeping on.

Forgiveness, oh yes, forgiveness.

9
How would others be impacted if I killed myself?

My brother Gary's suicide is still embedded in my mind, and I experience periods of regret to this day, which makes me very sad. I have to accept the fact that the memory of it will never go away.

Gary was four years younger than me and was an Army combat engineer in Vietnam. He was part of a team that moved into neutral or enemy territory and made it ready for later teams of soldiers to be protected by a little fortress, so to speak. It was dangerous work.

When he returned home from Nam, about 1968, he moved in with our parents on Whitegate Avenue in Sunland, CA., still within the city limits of Los Angeles. Gary was a tough guy. He started a gang called The Eagles, and twice I took him to an emergency room—once to get his jaw wired and once to do the same to a wrist. All the Philpott boys were boxers; my dad trained us to do this when we were very young. I still pound the body bag and work the speed bag every Wednesday at the gym. Our brother Bruce ended his career in policing as chief of police of Pasadena. After he died, we found boxing trophies in his closet, won in a boxing league formed by LA cops plus the county's sheriff's department.

Gary and I were very close, and I blame myself for not acting when we found out he shot himself in the hand. My parents were very concerned and started getting him help at an Army hospital. But one day, early in the morning, he drove to a Lutheran Hospital in San Fernando Valley, parked his VW Beetle under an American flag, and shot himself in the head. My mom, dad, brother, and I were shocked to the core, and we each blamed ourselves for not taking action earlier.

You can see where I am going with this. Yes, what would my family members—my five kids, eight grand kids, and three great grand kids go through, if their relative and a long-time pastor killed himself? Then my ex-wives, my present wife, and all my friends at the church, all the kids I coached at high schools in Marin here, and more as well—how would my suicide impact them? Certainly not for good, and some likely very badly.

Right now, I am sitting here typing this, and I am not feeling good at all. I am almost shattered to even think like this. To be truthful, I started to write this little booklet almost fourteen years ago, but always seemed to find ways not to finish it. The potential impact on others is likely the number one reason that I am stopped in really considering doing myself in. I may seem like a real basket case to you right now, dear reader, but let me say that I am far stronger now in my desire to continue living than ever before. Please do not worry about me.

I am putting this little chapter toward the end of this booklet to avoid upsetting any reader. But it is this reason, the possibility that killing myself would hurt and damage others who know and love me, that operates the most powerfully. Especially my dear daughters and son would be shattered and would never get over it.

Also, I am presenting this chapter so that others who might be considering doing away with themselves would stop and think about how this would trouble others—those who love and know you—even those whom you do not feel good about.

Now then, as we near the conclusion of this short series of essays, if you are mired in a desire to kill yourself, stop and think it over. Give a stalwart family member or friend a call and start talking with them, being real about what is going on in your head and heart. You do not have to feel embarrassed about this; it takes courage and strength to reach out for help.

Feeling, thinking, or planning to take your own life is not at all unusual, especially in this crazy mixed-up world of ours. I mean, it goes with the territory. To have thoughts or a desire to end it all is not surprising, and I would guess that a sizeable percentage of the population today is experiencing such things, especially the young people. You would be surprised if you knew how many of the people you know are going through some rough spots.

Last Sunday at church, we had a congregational meeting following the morning service. At one point, while making a summary of what was coming up, I talked about writing this book. And wow, so many looked at me and nodded their heads in agreement. Turns out, I was not the only one who had these disabling ideas in his head. It was at that point, with the heads nodding and a couple of thumbs up, that I knew this little book had to get out.

10
Their Stories

Following are a few stories sent to me by people I know or with whom I have had some contact. Maybe you can relate to something in one of them, and you will gain some peace for your own situation.

Carla's Story

(Author's note: Carla was a participant in our Divorce Recovery and Loss Workshop in the mid-1990s. She attended two workshops, each eight weeks long, back-to-back, volunteered as a small group facilitator, and showed up sporadically for a couple years after that, which is a typical pattern. She now works in the mental health field.)

It's funny that in my situation I was the one who left; I was the dumper. Quickly, too quickly, I jumped into a rebound relationship, and when that one came to its inevitable end, I crashed. I felt the full force of being alone in the world and was not prepared for it.

I left my marriage because of emotional and verbal abuse. I left because my twenty-year marriage was actually a combat zone. The issue was his desire to control me and my passive compliance. Eventually, I no longer cared if the wolves came and gnawed the flesh off my bones. I just had to go.

When I woke up alone in the world, I saw no hope for my future. I was sure I would die alone, but only after many years of suffering. I was depressed, and I began to think about suicide. I remembered something from the recovery workshop—90% of the people who go through divorce seriously consider ending it all.

At that point, it was helpful to me that I had children, college age, and I didn't want to scare them. I was motivated to get myself together for them. The other piece of it was that somehow I knew things were as bad as they were going to get and that I might at least try and see what would happen if I tried to make it better. I can't really explain it better than that.

Slowly I started reaching out. I went to therapy, Alanon, and divorce recovery workshop. I read books on relationship addiction and on why women stay too long in abusive situations. I worked the 12 Steps of Alanon for family members of alcoholics. I opened myself up to positive feedback, and I let others tell me good things about myself. I learned to pray and meditate. I embraced nature and beauty wherever I could find it. I complimented strangers. I said yes when I was invited into a women's group through Alanon. I volunteered at our local abused women's shelter. I started living a life I had never lived before. I learned that I belonged in the world for the first time. I sponsored other women in Alanon, and I became a facilitator at the divorce recovery workshop. I went to graduate school and got my masters degree in psychology.

I am actually grateful for the dark days, because I saw at that point that I had nothing more to lose, and I just starting taking small steps towards making it a little better. And I have never looked back.

Joan's Story

In 1974, Frank came home and found the gas furnace on with the pilot light off. His remark was, "What are you trying to do, kill everyone?" It was an innocent enough statement for his standpoint, but I had never let him know that I was struggling with a second severe post-partum depression and had for several months contemplated suicide.

I could see no way out of the darkness. I did not want to leave the children behind, so I wanted them to die with me. But I could not figure out how to take them with me yet not hurt them at the same time. What confusion and despair I was in. My thinking so crazy but I could not muddle through it.

I couldn't talk to Frank, but soon after that episode I found wonderful compassionate therapists who recognized that I was severely depressed. I met with my therapists several times a week and had to call in every night. They stood by me until my brain chemistry returned to normal.

I have learned that I do not manage anger very well. I tend to withdraw instead of dealing with it or just letting it go. When I begin to recognize the early stages of depression, I ask myself what I am angry about. It's not about someone else, it's about ME. I may be procrastinating, or my life may be out of balance. I may feel powerless. I look at what I can change and what cannot be changed. I like to say to myself, "Don't be sad…be mad."

Really, I didn't decide not to kill myself or the children. I just did not want to leave the children and I did not want to hurt them. I was fortunate enough to find the right therapists who would listen non-judgmentally and teach me about depression. For twenty years I lived with the fear and shame of what I might have done.

Eddie's Story

(Author's Note: Eddie was an inmate at San Quentin Prison. He received a long sentence under California's Three Strike law. He was essentially a non-violent offender. After receiving a substantial inheritance from his father, he became addicted to cocaine, and after the money ran out, he committed two burglaries at relative's homes and earned three counts. He had rather radical surgery to survive cancer after which he was no longer able to play baseball for the Giants, but when he could he was an excellent second baseman and leadoff hitter. Eddie is a solid Christian and lives it the best he can. Here in his own words is his story.)

My name is Eddie Robinson. I am in prison for stealing money to get high. My sentence is fifty years to life. This year (2010) is number 16, and so far, I have been placed on suicide watch four different times.

I am learning with each suicide attempt that what I am fighting is my reality and the fairness of life. Life is not fair when a murderer goes home before a petty criminal like me—it's not fair. Yet it's my reality. My reality is that I'm in prison with no chance of being released until the year 2044 when I will be given my first chance at parole. (Note: Due to amazing circumstances not related here, Eddie did get out of San Quentin ten years after writing this.)

Suicide seems to be my way of taking control. For whatever reason I have not killed myself, and I do not know even today why I do not. Sitting in my cell just now, death seems better than facing the next 37 years in prison.

My life is a lonely one, and often angry, wondering what I've done in my life to bring such misery. I cannot imagine reality being any worse.

Then there are days when I'm able to accept life, accept prison, and accept my reality and all that God brings my way. It is on those days I notice I'm happy, even smiling, able to breathe and see God's beauty. And if I can do this in prison, I know it's possible for anyone else to do it, too. Let life have its way. It's going to anyway.

Sharon's Story

(Author's Note: Below is a small excerpt from Sharon Dutra's story. I interviewed her along with her husband Mike a few years ago. They have produced a fabulous 16-minute video and gave the link to it to put in this book. It can be found on YouTube at):

https://www.youtube.com/watch?v=UuH8U_dRdiw&t=21s

I never imagined that I would end up living on the street for two years. I was that proverbial "bag lady" you often see on the street. I lived in a predominantly black neighborhood when I was homeless, and I would go up into the projects at night for drugs – which is something even the locals wouldn't do because it was so dangerous. I occasionally scoured garbage cans for food, but I usually just sold my body so I could survive and keep up my drug habit. I certainly had a death wish. Twice, guns were pulled on me, and once I told the guy "Shoot me and put me out of my misery". I tried to commit suicide on several occasions, but I couldn't even succeed at that. I was miraculously spared from death on so many occasions. It's funny – when you're "out there" – you just don't realize how "out there" you really are until you get your life back.

11
Concluding Thoughts

I am glad I decided not to kill myself. How close did I come to it? Likely unanswerable.

I am also glad you read this little book and that you have the strength to look at reality. It takes emotional strength to face such a thing.

Last, I want to state again the reason for this piece: if I could be up front and admit what I went through, so can you. To "fess up" does not mean you are weak or a basket case. Not at all! Just the opposite, since it reveals that you have the ability to face difficult issues and talk about them.

Suggestion: keep this booklet handy, as you might find someone else to give it to.

Also:

There is a national suicide and crisis number as well: 988. It is 988lifeline.org, which is a Suicide & Crisis Lifeline.

Another help line is titled "warm," and it can be reached by typing into a browser: warmline.org. Try it; it is very helpful.

Some states have help lines, too. Here in California it is Cal help.

www.ingramcontent.com/pod-product-compliance
Lightning Source LLC
Chambersburg PA
CBHW041327110526
44592CB00021B/2845